Discovering 2-D Shapes in Art

Julia Wall

Real World Math Books are published by Capstone Press,
151 Good Counsel Drive, P.O. Box 669, Mankato, Minnesota 56002.
www.capstonepress.com

122009
005647WZS10

Books published by Capstone Press are manufactured with paper
containing at least 10 percent post-consumer waste.

Library of Congress Cataloging-in-Publication Data
Wall, Julia.
  Discovering 2-D shapes in art / by Julia Wall. -- 1st hardcover ed.
     p. cm. -- (Real world math)
  Includes index.
  ISBN 978-1-4296-5188-2 (lib. bdg.)
  1. Geometry in art--Juvenile literature. 2. Shapes--Juvenile literature. 3. Problem solving--Juvenile
     literature. I. Title. II. Title: Discovering two-D shapes in art.
  N72.M3W35 2009
   701'.8--dc22

2009051382

Editorial Credits
Sara Johnson, editor; Emily R. Smith, M.A.Ed., editorial director; Sharon Coan, M.S.Ed., editor-in-chief;
Lee Aucoin, creative director; Rachelle Cracchiolo, M.S.Ed., publisher

Photo Credits
The author and publisher would like to gratefully credit or acknowledge the following for permission
to reproduce copyright material: cover © Big Stock Photo/ Ron Sumners; title © Big Stock Photo/Joan
Soles; p. 4 © photolibrary.com; p. 6 (above) © Alamy; p. 6 (below) © Wikipedia; p. 7 © 2008 Mondrian/
Holtzman Trust c/o HCR International, Virginia USA; p. 8 © The Art Archive / Tate Gallery London /
Eileen Tweedy; p. 9 © akg-images/CDA/Guillemot; p. 10 © photolibrary.com; p. 11 © Big Stock Photo/
Dawn Allynn; p. 13 © Big Stock Photo/ Ron Sumners; p. 15 © Rob Cruse; p. 16 © Big Stock Photo/
Kimberly Greenleaf; p. 17 © Big Stock Photo/ Aravind Teki; p. 22 © Shutterstock/ Amy Nichole Harris;
p. 23 © Big Stock Photo/ Loredana Bell; p. 24–27 © Lindsay Edwards Photography; p. 28 © Big Stock
Photo/ Margie Hurwich.

While every care has been taken to trace and acknowledge copyright, the publishers tender their
apologies for any accidental infringement where copyright has proved untraceable. They would be
pleased to come to a suitable arrangement with the rightful owner in each case.

Table of Contents

Shapes All Around

Look around your school. What shapes can you see? Can you see squares, triangles, or rectangles? These are all 2-D shapes.

Most 2-D shapes have length and width. Each of these is a **dimension** (duh-MEN-shuhn). 2-D is short for two-dimensional.

What Are 2-D Shapes?

2-D shapes are flat shapes that you can draw. There are two types of 2-D shapes, polygons and non-polygons.

Polygons have straight sides. All of the sides and **angles** are equal in a **regular** polygon.

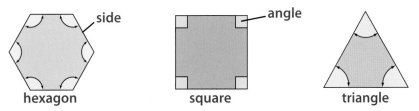

hexagon   square   triangle

Irregular polygons have sides or angles that are not all equal.

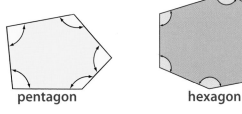

pentagon   hexagon

Non-polygons are shapes that have a curved side.

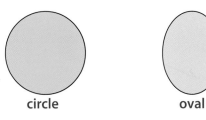

circle   oval

Shapes in Art

You can find 2-D shapes in art. 2-D shapes are used in paintings. You can also see them in **sculptures** (SKULP-churs) and in **mosaics** (mo-ZAY-iks).

These mosaic benches were designed by Antonio Gaudi. They are in Barcelona, Spain.

LET'S EXPLORE MATH

Look at this flag.

a. Name the red 2-D shape.

b. Name another 2-D shape you can see.

c. What 2-D shape is the whole flag?

Paintings

This painting has squares and rectangles. The artist was thinking about Broadway, a busy part of New York.

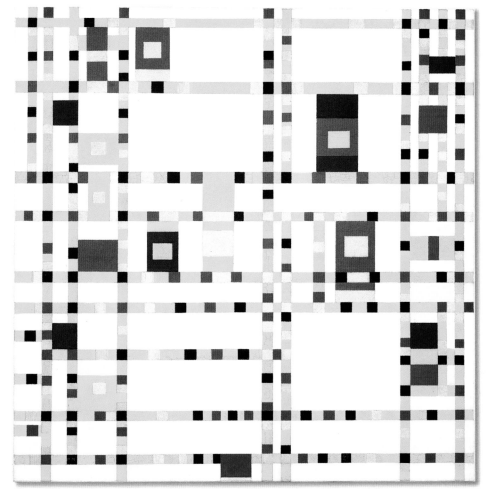

Mondrian, Piet (1872-1944) Broadway Boogie Woogie. 1942-43. Oil on canvas, 50 x 50".
© 2008 Mondrian/Holtzman Trust c/o HCR International, Virginia U.S.A.

This painting is called *Broadway Boogie Woogie*.

This painting is made up of irregular 2-D shapes. The shapes are in a **spiral**. The spiral is supposed to be a snail's shell.

This painting is called *The Snail*.

© Desc: L'Escargot Artist: Matisse, Henri: 1869–1954: French

Cubist Art

Cubism is a famous art form. Some cubist art uses 2-D shapes. Often, the shapes are broken up. They are put together again to make a picture.

Sculpture

What 2-D shapes can you see in this sculpture?
Louise Nevelson, an American sculptor, made it.

This sculpture is
made of wood.

Nevelson , Louise 1899 (or 1900)–1987. "Sky Cathedral III", 1960. (Assemblage made from 95 parts).
Wood relief, painted. 300 x 354 cm. Private collection.

LET'S EXPLORE MATH

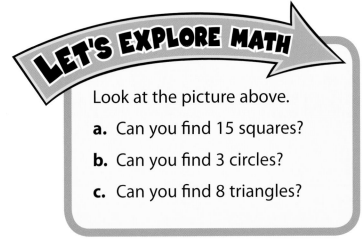

Look at the picture above.

a. Can you find 15 squares?

b. Can you find 3 circles?

c. Can you find 8 triangles?

Stained-Glass Windows

Look at this window. It is called a stained-glass window. It is in a church in France. Do you see any 2-D shapes?

This window is 40 feet (12 m) wide!

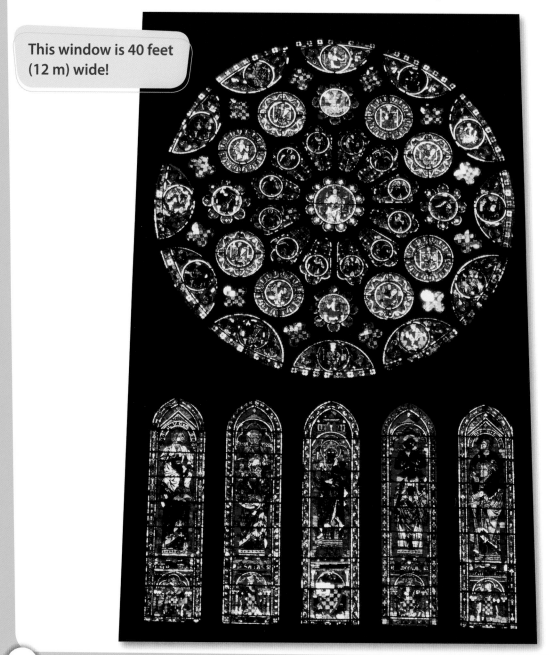

Look at all the shapes and patterns in this window. Squares, rectangles, and triangles are some of the 2-D shapes found in the window.

Patterns in Art

Shapes can fit together to make **tessellations** (teh-suh-LAY-shuhns). Tessellations make patterns. The shapes fit together with no gaps.

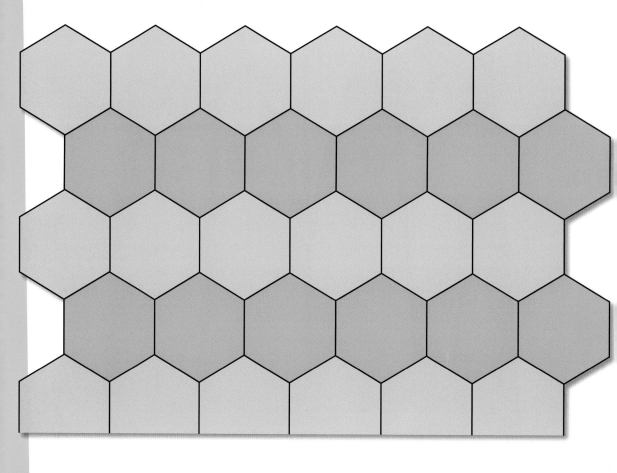

These hexagons fit together with no gaps.

Mosaics

Look at this mosaic. It is made up of small pieces of tile. Mosaics are sometimes used on buildings or pavements.

What shapes can you see in this mosaic?

LET'S EXPLORE MATH

Use a triangle to make a tessellating pattern.

a. Draw the triangle on cardboard and cut it out.

b. Trace around your triangle.

c. Turn, flip, or slide the cardboard triangle and trace around it again.

d. Continue moving your triangle to make a pattern with no gaps or overlaps.

e. Color your tessellation using 2 different colors.

Lines of Symmetry

Some shapes have lines of **symmetry**. Look at these 2-D shapes. If you fold them along these lines, each half is exactly the same.

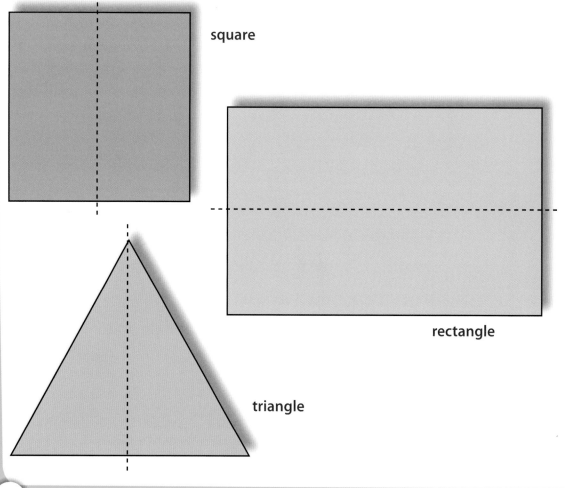

square

rectangle

triangle

The lines of symmetry are where you make the folds. These lines are also called mirror lines. If you place a mirror on the lines, you can see the whole shape.

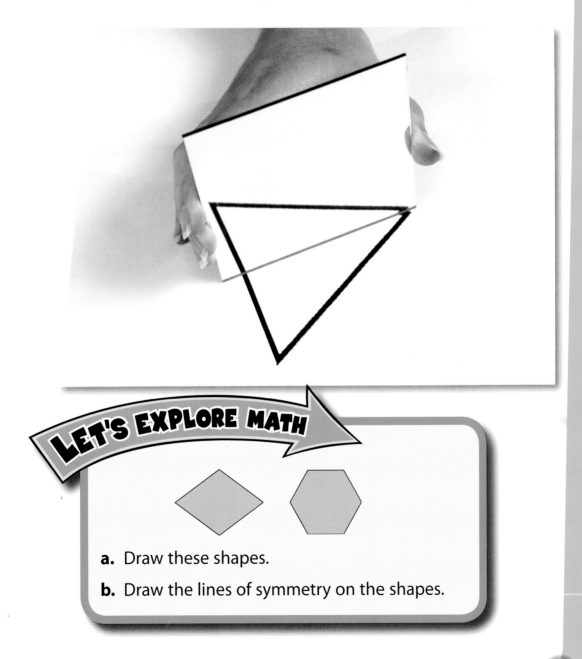

LET'S EXPLORE MATH

a. Draw these shapes.

b. Draw the lines of symmetry on the shapes.

Symmetry in Art

Symmetrical Mosaics

Many artists use symmetry in their work. Patterns can be symmetrical, too. Can you see the lines of symmetry in this mosaic?

Some 2-D shapes can have more than 1 line of symmetry.

Symmetrical Architecture

Architects (AR-kuh-tekts) also use symmetry in their buildings. The Taj Mahal (tahj muh-HAHL) in India is famous for its symmetry and shapes.

The floors and walkways in the Taj Mahal have tiles in tessellated patterns.

Tangrams

A tangram is a puzzle. It has 7 pieces that fit together to make a square shape. The idea is to make a picture with these 7 pieces.

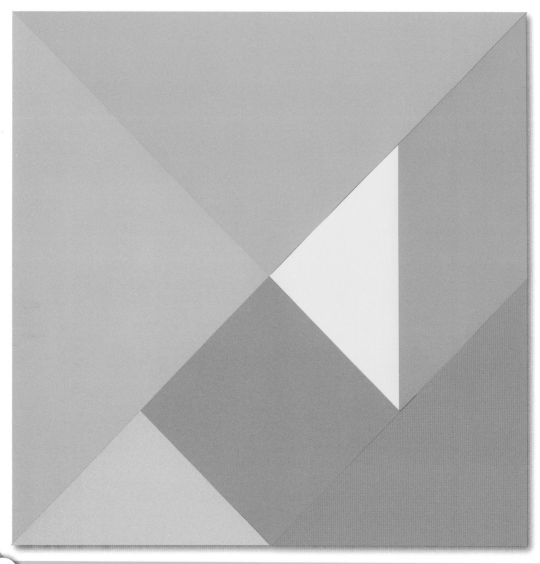

A Closer Look

So what are the 7 shapes in the tangram?
There are 5 triangles, 1 square, and 1 **parallelogram**.

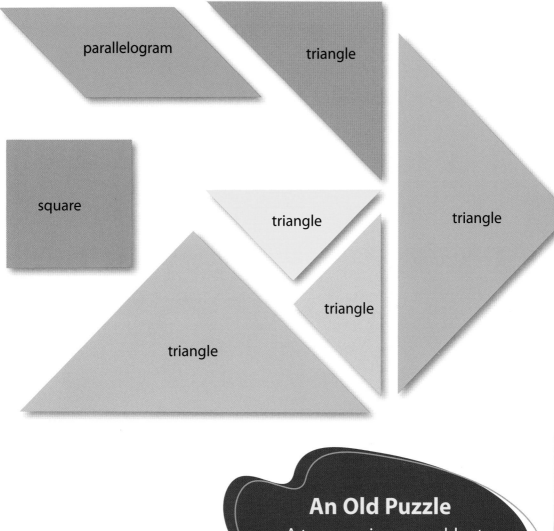

parallelogram

triangle

square

triangle

triangle

triangle

triangle

An Old Puzzle
A tangram is a very old art
form that comes from China.

Tangram Art

Look at this picture made from a tangram.
It looks easy to do, doesn't it?

Now it's your turn! Draw your own tangram square and cut out the shapes. (Use pages 18–19 as a guide.)

Can you make this dinosaur shape?

LET'S EXPLORE MATH

Use your tangram pieces to complete these puzzles:

a. Make a large triangle out of the medium triangle and 2 small triangles.

b. Make a large triangle using the square and 2 small triangles.

c. Make a parallelogram using 2 small triangles.

d. Make a large triangle using the parallelogram and 2 small triangles.

Art Where You Live

Shapes are all around us. Take a walk through your neighborhood or city. Look at the buildings around you.

These buildings are in Shanghai, China.

Art is everywhere, too. Visit an art **gallery** if you can. You will see wonderful paintings. You might also see mosaics and sculptures.

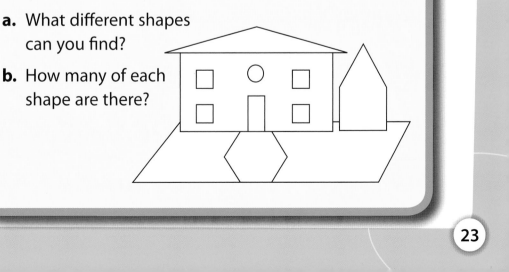

LET'S EXPLORE MATH

Look at this picture.

a. What different shapes can you find?

b. How many of each shape are there?

Make Your Own Work of Art

Now you can use shapes to make your own art. Let's make a colored window. You can use colored shapes to do this.

First, think what you want your window to look like. Draw a pattern of shapes on your "window frame." You might draw circles and squares.

Next, cut out the shapes from the frame. Then cut out shapes of colored paper. Tape the colored paper over the frame.

Stick your art on a window. You have made a beautiful piece of art!

LET'S EXPLORE MATH

a. Which of these shapes are regular 2-D shapes? Why?

b. Which of these shapes are irregular 2-D shapes? Why?

The Final Straw

It's a rainy day outside and Soula is bored. Her mom has just come back from the grocery store. Soula decides to help her mom unpack the groceries. Mom has bought a packet of drinking straws for a barbecue on the weekend. The packet contains 25 straws all the same length.

Soula decides to use the straws to make shapes on the kitchen table.

Solve It!

a. Soula has 25 straws all the same length. How many triangles and squares can Soula make with her straws? She has to use all the straws without having any left over.

b. Do the problem again and make a different number of triangles and squares. (You can have straws left over.)

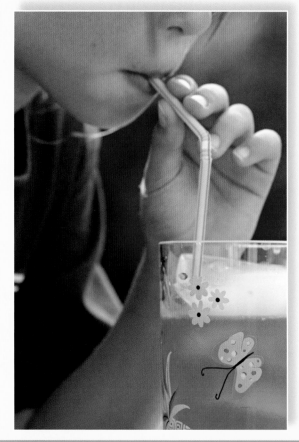

Use these steps to help you solve the problems.

Step 1: Draw 25 lines to represent the straws.

Step 2: Draw a square. Cross off the number of lines you used.

Step 3: Draw a triangle. Cross off the number of lines you used.

Step 4: For problem a. continue drawing squares and triangles, crossing off the lines until there are no lines left over. For problem b. you may have some lines left over.

Glossary

angles—the amounts of turning between two joined-up lines

architects—people who design, or draw, buildings

dimension—the measurement of a shape; 2-D shapes have width and length.

gallery—a place where works of art are stored and displayed

irregular—not regular; an irregular shape has sides and angles that are not equal.

mosaics—artworks made from small pieces of colored glass, stone, or clay

parallelogram—a four-sided 2-D shape with opposite sides and angles that are equal

regular—having all sides equal and all angles equal

sculptures—artworks made by modeling, carving, or constructing shapes from clay, stone, wood, or metal

spiral—a curve that becomes smaller and smaller toward the center

symmetry—having the same size and shape across a line

tessellations—repeating patterns of shapes that fit together with no gaps and no overlaps

Index

Internet Sites

FactHound offers a safe, fun way to find Internet sites related to this book. All of the sites on FactHound have been researched by our staff.

Here's all you do:

Visit *www.facthound.com*

FactHound will fetch the best sites for you!

Let's Explore Math

Page 6:

a. Triangle

b. A star

c. A rectangle

Page 9:

Answers will vary.

Page 13:

Answers will vary but may show a pattern like the one below.

Page 15:

Page 21:

a. **b.** **c.** **d.**

Page 23:

a. Circle, triangle, squares, rectangles, pentagon, hexagon.

b. 1 circle (above door); 1 triangle (roof); 4 squares (windows) 2 rectangles (house, and door); 1 pentagon (building next to house); 1 hexagon (garden path) 1 parallelogram (land).

Page 27:

a. The square and the triangle are regular 2-D shapes because they have equal sides and equal angles.

b. The hexagon and the pentagon are irregular 2-D shapes because their sides and angles are not equal.

Problem-Solving Activity:

a. Soula can make 4 squares and 3 triangles.

b. Answers will vary but could include 4 triangles and 3 squares with 1 straw left over.